D1226354

Adorable
Accessories

Paper Creations to Wear

by Jennifer Phillips

CAPSTONE PRESS
a capstone imprint

Table *of* Contents

Fold it.
Tear it.
Make it.
Wear it.

That's right—you can wear paper! Take your wardrobe from drab to fab with the amazing paper creations in this book. Add color to your outfit with a braided paper scarf. Use paper to pump up your kicks. Or use paper jewelry to glam up your look.

Ready to get rolling? Start by gathering paper. You can find colorful paper and printed card stock at craft and office supply stores. But papers such as sheet music, maps, or wrapping paper are great options too. Next get those craft tools ready. You probably already have basic paper craft tools such as scissors, rulers, and craft glue. Any supplies you don't have can be found at most hardware, craft, or office supply stores.

So what are you waiting for? Get paper crafting, and make some accessories your friends will go crazy over!

1 tape measure
2 hot glue gun
3 slotted quilling tool
4 craft knife
5 quilling needle
6 pliers
7 decoupage glue
8 compass
9 craft glue

5

Butterfly Necklace

Let your creativity take flight with this pretty piece. It truly will be the centerpiece of any outfit.

1. Draw the outline of a butterfly that's about 3 inches (8 centimeters) wide on poster board. (If drawing isn't your thing, you can find butterfly templates online to trace.) Then cut out the butterfly shape.

2. Lightly sketch designs on the butterfly wings, such as long ovals. Carefully cut out the patterns with a craft knife.

3. Spray paint the butterfly on one side. Let dry. Then repeat on the other side.

4. Follow the directions on the can to spray the butterfly on both sides with sealant. Let dry.

5. Use the sharp point of the craft knife to cut a tiny hole in the bottom center of the butterfly's body. Thread a jump ring through the hole. Attach hanging beads to the jump ring.

6. Use the knife point to cut tiny holes in the top left and right wing tips. Thread jump rings through these holes, and use them to connect the chain to the wings.

7. Glue jewel beads to the butterfly's wings and body for added sparkle.

Tip: Use a sharp craft knife to make sure the butterfly doesn't have ragged edges.

Ring Bling

Add a splash of color to any outfit with this spectacular ring, and let the fun blossom.

1. Measure the length around your finger. Add ½ inch (1 cm). This is the length of your cardboard piece. Then decide how slender or chunky you want your ring band. Cut a rectangle of cardboard in the dimensions you need.

2. Paint both sides of your cardboard piece. Let dry.

3. Brush decoupage glue over both sides of the cardboard piece, and let dry.

4. Wrap the cardboard band around your finger to get a correct fit. Hot glue the ends together, overlapping enough to create a strong seam. Let dry.

5. Use the compass to draw a 2-inch (5-cm) circle on decorative paper. Cut out the circle.

6. Use the compass to lightly draw a ½-inch (1-cm) circle in the center of the paper circle.

7. Cut the outside edge of the circle in strips, stopping at the center circle. Bend up every other strip slightly to create two layers of petals.

8. Hot glue a bead in the center of the flower.

9. Hot glue the flower to the ring.

10. Follow the directions on the can to spray the ring and flower with sealant. Let dry.

Materials:

tape measure

single-ply cardboard

small paint brushes

acrylic paints

decoupage glue

hot glue

math compass

decorative paper

1 bead

clear acrylic gloss coating sealant

Tip: For the cardboard, try coffee cup sleeves or look for decorative border rolls found in craft, party, and teacher supply stores.

Dangling Decorations

Can't find the perfect earrings? Then make them! You can use just about any kind of paper for these accessories. So get creative, and let your personality shine!

Materials:

½- or ¾-inch (1- or 2-cm) circle paper punch

patterned paper, such as maps, sheet music, or decorative scrapbook paper

glue stick

solid color paper

foam brush

decoupage glue

clear acrylic gloss coating sealant

needle

4 thin wire jump rings

2 earring hooks

1. Punch four circles from the patterned paper. Glue together two circles with the pattern sides facing out. Repeat with the other two circles.

2. Punch four circles from the solid color paper. On each circle, make one cut from the edge to the center.

3. Brush decoupage glue on one side of each circle. Let dry. Repeat on the other side.

4. Follow the directions on the can to spray the circles with sealant. Spray one side and let dry. Then repeat for the other side.

5. Use a needle to poke top and bottom holes in the patterned circles a little bit from the edges. Poke a top hole in two of the plain circles.

6. Thread a jump ring through the hole in one of the plain circles. Then thread the jump ring through the bottom hole of a patterned circle. Repeat for the second earring.

7. Run glue on the inside edges of the slit in one of the remaining plain circles. Slide the circle over one of the attached plain circles. Repeat with the other circle on the second earring. Let the glue dry.

8. Use jump rings to attach earring hooks to the tops of the patterned circles.

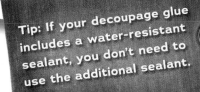

Tip: If your decoupage glue includes a water-resistant sealant, you don't need to use the additional sealant.

Heads Up

Transform a plain plastic headband into a personal style statement. You'll turn heads with this paper project.

1. Measure the length of the headband and the width from the narrowest to widest points. Don't include the band's rims.

2. Draw a template on copy paper that follows the headband's dimensions and shape. If your paper isn't long enough, create two halves. Lay the template over the headband, and trim to fit.

3. Trace the template on decorative paper. Then cut out the shape.

4. Brush glue on the headband. Lay the decorative paper piece on top, smoothing out any wrinkles. Let dry.

5. Glue ribbon to the edges of the headband. Make sure to fold the ribbon over the edge and glue it on the back too. Let dry.

6. Insert a paper strip into the slotted quilling tool. Hold the tool with your dominant hand, and rest the tool on your other hand's forefinger. Roll the tool to quill the paper. When you get to the end, hold the rolled strip securely using your thumb and middle finger. Push the paper roll off the tool.

7. Use the quilling needle to apply glue to the rolled paper end. Press and hold until secure.

8. Repeat steps 6–7 to make as many quilled shapes as you want. Be creative with the shapes. Some can be rolled completely. Roll just part of some strips, leaving a tail. Squeeze a rolled circle to create a teardrop. Keep some rolls tight, and let others get loose before gluing. Have fun!

9. Squeeze a small puddle of glue onto scrap paper. Carefully dip the bottom edges of a shape in glue. Place the shape on the headband. Gently press down on the shape to secure. Repeat for all the shapes.

10. Glue beads or jewels to the headband as accents.

11. Follow the directions on the can to spray the headband with sealant. Let dry.

Materials:

measuring tape

wide, plastic headband

copy paper

decorative paper

foam brush

craft glue

ribbon

quilling paper strips

slotted quilling tool

quilling needle

small beads or jewels

clear acrylic gloss coating sealant

Sassy Skirt

Don't toss out that skirt! Refresh its look, and design your own boutique fashion with pretty paper rosettes.

Materials:

crepe paper streamers

decorative-edge scissors

thread and sewing needle

clear acrylic gloss coating sealant

skirt

hot glue

beads

1. Cut a 19-inch (48-cm) length of crepe paper off the roll. Cut the paper in half lengthwise using decorative-edge scissors.

2. Thread a needle, and knot one end. Gently sew a line of stitches along the straight edge of one paper strip. Pull the thread tight as you go to create an accordion fold.

3. When you reach the end, stitch the strip's ends together. First sew up the ends, then stitch back down so the needle comes back to the stitched side.

4. Pinch the folds on the stitched side together. Run the needle through the pinched center several times to sew it together well. Knot the end of the thread and cut off the extra.

5. Pinching the stitched end, gently push the unstitched folds out flat and into a rosette shape.

6. Repeat steps 1–5 to create as many rosettes as you need.

7. Follow the directions on the can to spray the rosettes with sealant. Let dry.

8. Sew the bottom of the rosettes to your skirt. If your skirt has a built-in slip, run the needle and thread through the skirt only and not the slip.

9. Sew or hot glue beads in the centers of the flowers.

Tip: The rosettes will be water-resistant but regular washing is not recommended. Instead, use a home dry cleaning kit to clean this skirt.

Paper Purse

Keep your essentials in this fun paper purse for a day on the go. This project is so fun, you could make a new one to match every outfit!

Materials:

clear acrylic gloss coating sealant

3 12-inch (30-cm) square
double-sided
card stock sheets

strong fabric glue or hot glue

craft knife

an eyelet kit with 2 large eyelets

ribbon

1. Follow the directions on the can to spray both sides of the card stock sheets with sealant. Let dry.

2. Hold two card stock sheets together, pattern sides facing down. Use paper clips to keep the sheets together. Measure 1 inch (2.5 cm) from each top corner and make a mark. Then measure 2½ inches (6.4 cm) from the middle of the top edge. Make a mark there too. Draw a half circle from one edge mark to the other, with the deepest part reaching the middle mark. Cut along your pencil line. This is the top of the purse.

3. While the sheets are still clipped together, fold both sides over 1 inch (2.5 cm). Remove the clips.

Tip: For a different look, use a handle from an old purse instead of making a paper one.

4. Lay one cut sheet on your workspace, pattern side down and folded flaps standing up. Dot glue along one flap. Align the other sheet over the first sheet so the pattern side faces out. Press the flaps together, and glue in place. Repeat on the other side. Let dry.

5. Gently press the sides down to lay the purse shell flat. Fold the bottom of both sheets up 5 inches (13 cm) and crease. Unfold. Put your hand inside the purse shell and gently pop the sides back up.

6. Set the shell on your workspace with the curved top down. Gently press one bottom side in and down on the fold line. Crease the bottom flaps so they stay standing with the side pressed in. Repeat on the other side.

7. Fold the two bottom flaps in half lengthwise. Glue these flaps together as a bottom seam. Let dry.

8. Put your hand inside the purse and gently push the bottom out to sit flat.

9. To make the handle, cut two 2x12-inch (5x30-cm) strips from the third piece of card stock. On each strip, fold both long sides to the center, pattern side facing out. Apply glue underneath each fold and hold in place to dry. Overlap one end of each paper strip 1 inch (2.5 cm) and glue together. Use the craft knife to cut small holes 1 inch (2.5 cm) from each end.

10. Cut small holes on the sides of the purse, 1 inch (2.5 cm) from the top. Insert the eyelets through the holes in the handles and purse to connect them. Follow the directions with the kit to attach the eyelets. Smooth the handle into a curved shape.

11. Glue ribbon along the curved top edges to give the purse a finished look.

Pleated Flower Necklace

Head to the kitchen to get supplies for this project. Who knew baking cups could be this gorgeous?

Materials:

4 mini paper baking cups

foam brush

decoupage glue

hot glue

decorative beads and buttons

thick necklace chain

clear acrylic gloss coating sealant

1. Pinch together the bottom of a paper baking cup so the inner circle folds in tightly. Use your other hand to pull down the pleated paper edges into a circle. You can make this almost flat or keep some folds uneven.

2. Holding the folded bottom together, brush a thick layer of decoupage glue over the top pleats. Set the unglued side on a paper towel.

3. Repeat steps 1–2 with the other baking cups. Let them all dry.

Tip: Use more or fewer paper flowers on the necklace to fit your taste. It's your necklace, so do it your way!

4. Turn all the cups over and brush decoupage glue on the bottoms. Let dry.

5. Hot glue beads or buttons in the middle of each flower. Let dry.

6. Hot glue the flowers to the necklace chain wherever you wish. Let dry.

7. Fill in the gaps between the flowers by gluing buttons on the chain.

8. Follow the directions on the can to spray both sides of the necklace with sealant. Let dry.

Lucky Stars

Make your wish for fantastic accessories come true with these shining stars. Be ready for lots of attention with these eye-catching creations.

1. Cut two ½x12-inch (1x30-cm) paper strips.

2. Follow this folding sequence to create a star:

   - Start with one strip of paper colored side down. Tie a knot in the left end of the strip. Carefully tighten the knot.

   - There will be a short piece on the left of the knot. Tuck this piece under the top layer of the knot. The result should be a pentagon shape with a point at the top.

   - Wrap the long end of the strip tightly around and around the pentagon sides, following the natural path the paper wants to take.

   - When you have just a bit of paper left, tuck it snugly into the top layer of the knot.

   - Hold the edges of the knot between your fingers and thumbs. Use a fingernail to gently press in each side of the knot. The indented sides will cause the middle of the knot to puff up.

3. Repeat step 2 to create a second star.

4. Follow the directions on the can to spray both stars with sealant. Let dry.

5. Pierce a hole in the bottom and top point of each star with the sewing needle. Run an earring pin through each star so the loop hangs from the bottom.

6. Use a pliers to create a loop at the top of each pin and connect to the earring hooks. Attach hanging beads to the bottoms.

Materials:

wrapping paper

clear acrylic gloss coating sealant

heavy sewing needle

2 1½-inch (4-cm) long earring pins with a loop at one end

needle nose pliers

2 earring hooks

hanging beads

Tip: Practice makes perfect. Try making a few stars with plain paper before using the perfect paper for your earrings.

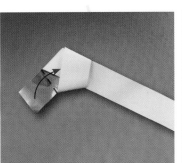
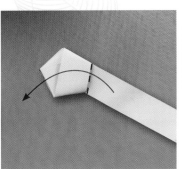
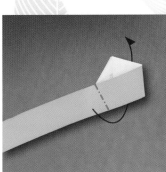

Hats Off

Top off your look with this fun crinkly hat made from tissue paper. It's the perfect accessory for your unique style!

1. Cover the hat in a tight layer of plastic wrap. Make sure the wrap follows the shape of the hat.

2. Cover just the top of the hat with a thin coating of cooking spray.

3. Brush a thin layer of decoupage glue on the sprayed part of the hat. Lay pieces of tissue paper on top of the glue, edges overlapping. Brush another thin layer of decoupage on top of the paper.

4. Continue covering the hat with tissue paper, working one small section at a time. Start by applying cooking spray to a small area. Then apply decoupage, tissue paper, then more decoupage. When finished, let the hat dry for several hours.

5. Cover the hat with another layer of tissue paper and decoupage. You don't need to use the cooking spray this time. When done, let the hat dry for several hours.

6. Repeat step 5.

7. Starting with the underside of the brim, carefully separate the tissue paper hat from the plastic-wrapped mold.

8. Follow the directions on the can to spray sealant on the hat. Let dry.

9. The hat will be pliable so you can shape it as needed. Trim the edge of the brim if needed to create a tidy look. Add a tie, yarn, or ribbon around the brim for extra flair.

Materials:

a fedora, small brimmed panama, or bowler style hat to use as a mold

plastic wrap

cooking spray

foam brush

decoupage glue

tissue paper, torn into pieces

clear acrylic gloss coating sealant

a tie, yarn, or ribbon

Belt It Out

Jazz up your outfits with a funky belt assembled from any mix of paper. Show off your wild side or go more subdued—it's up to you!

1. Measure your waist and add at least 4 inches (10 cm). This is the belt's length.

2. Decide how narrow or wide you want the belt to be. Measure the belt loops on your pants if you'll be wearing the belt that way.

3. Cut a strip of shelf liner in the dimensions you need.

4. Lay out the shelf liner with the pattern facing down. Cut strips of decorative paper that are the same width as the belt. Arrange the strips on the shelf liner. At this point, nothing will be stuck down, so you can rearrange all you want.

5. Once you're happy with the arrangement, move the decorative strips off the shelf liner. Keep the strips in order so you don't forget the plan! Peel off the protective paper on the liner to expose the sticky side.

6. Use spray adhesive to attach the decorative strips to the shelf liner paper. The liner is sticky, but the adhesive gives a permanent hold.

7. Trim away any paper backing peeking out around the belt.

8. Follow the directions on the can to spray the belt with sealant. Let dry.

9. Decide what will be a comfortable fit, and hot glue the magnets to the belt's ends. Glue one magnet inside and one out, so the belt will snap closed. Hot glue a decorative belt buckle or button on the outside front.

Materials:

tape measure

decorative shelf liner

decorative paper

multi-purpose spray adhesive

clear acrylic gloss coating sealant

hot glue

2 small, thin craft magnets

lightweight belt buckle or buttons

Tip: You can use almost any type of paper for this belt. Some ideas include: mini playing cards, small gift tags, bookmarks, Chinese gift envelopes, decorative napkins, wrapping paper, play money, or book pages.

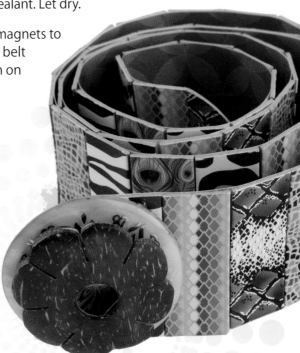

Paper Scarf

Wrap yourself in this sophisticated accessory. It looks sleek and trendy, but it's super easy to make.

1. Carefully separate the layers of each paper tablecloth. Put one layer of each color on your workspace. Set the other layers aside.

2. Cut the three layers to each be 18 inches (46 cm) wide. Cut them to the length you want your scarf to be.

3. Get one of the layers you set aside. Cut two 1x12-inch (2.5x30-cm) strips from this layer. Fold each pipe cleaner inside a strip. Glue the pipe cleaner to the inside edges of the paper.

4. Lay one of the long tablecloth pieces on a flat surface. Gently roll it lengthwise into a loose cylinder. Then accordion fold it lengthwise to create soft pleats. Repeat with the other two tablecloth pieces.

5. Lay the three tablecloth pieces side by side with the ends even. Gather them together 6 inches (15 cm) from one end. Wrap a covered pipe cleaner around the layers to hold them together.

6. Loosely braid the three tablecloths together. Secure them together 6 inches (15 cm) from the other end with another pipe cleaner.

7. Follow the directions on the can to spray sealant on the scarf. Let dry.

Beaded Bracelet

Wear your heart on your sleeve! Use papers that are close to your heart to make beads for this beautiful bracelet. You'll be able to show off your personality and style all at once.

1. Cut 16 triangles from the paper. Each triangle should be 10 inches (25 cm) long and 1 inch (2.5 cm) wide on one side.

2. Put one triangle on your workspace, pattern side down. Rub glue on the triangle.

3. Put a skewer on the wide edge of the triangle. Roll the paper tightly around the stick. Glue down the tip, and slide the bead off the skewer. Repeat to create a total of 16 paper beads. If the skewer starts to get gummy from the glue, clean it off or use a new one.

4. Follow the directions on the can to spray sealant on the beads. Roll the beads to cover all sides. Let dry.

5. Thread the elastic cord through one paper bead so it's centered in the middle of the cord.

Materials:

decorative paper, such as sheet music, comics, maps, or your own artwork

glue stick

wooden skewers

clear acrylic gloss coating sealant

9 feet (3 meters) of elastic bracelet cord

25–30 ¼-inch (.6-cm) or larger round beads

6. Thread the left end of the string through a second paper bead. Place that bead on your workspace parallel to the first bead. Both ends of the string will be on the right side.

7. Grab the string from the first bead. Put one round bead on this string. Then thread the string back through the second paper bead going left. You'll now have one string coming out both sides of the second paper bead. The round bead will create an edge between the paper beads.

8. Repeat steps 6 and 7, adding one round bead before the paper bead on the left side. Add another bead before you thread the string back over on the right side. Pull the ends tight as you work to keep the beads laying together flat.

9. When the bracelet is the length you need, add a final set of round beads on each side. Do this as you run the string ends through the first paper bead. Tie the cord's ends together in a tight knot. Cut off the extra string. Depending on the size of your wrist, you might not use all the beads or you might need more.

29

Fancy Footwear

Take a creative stand. Turn a pair of plain shoes into fashion flair. These shoes are an accessory you can't go without.

1. Peel away the inside plain layers of the decorative napkins. Cut the decorated layers into strips.

2. Brush decoupage glue on a section of a shoe. Position a napkin strip as desired. Trim the strip if needed. Once it's the way you like, brush a thin layer of decoupage on top. Repeat in sections around both shoes until you're finished. Let dry.

3. Brush another layer of decoupage glue on the shoes. Let dry.

4. Follow the directions on the can to spray the shoes with sealant. Let them dry completely before wearing.

Materials:

decorative napkins or other decorative paper

foam brush

decoupage glue

a pair of shoes with a smooth surface

clear acrylic gloss coating sealant

Tip: You can use just about any paper for this project. Instead of napkins, try gluing on pictures cut from magazines or books.

Read More

Phillips, Jennifer. *Snappy Style: Paper Decoration Creations*. Paper Creations. North Mankato, Minn.: Capstone Press, 2013.

Stevens-Heebner, Marty. *Altered Shoes: A Step-by-Step Guide to Making Your Footwear Fabulous*. Cincinnati, Ohio: Krause Publications, 2009.

Terry, Kayte. *Paper Made!: 101 Exceptional Projects to Make Out of Everyday Paper*. New York: Workman Pub., 2012.

Internet Sites

FactHound offers a safe, fun way to find Internet sites related to this book. All of the sites on FactHound have been researched by our staff.

Here's all you do:

Visit *www.facthound.com*

Type in this code: 9781620650431

Check out projects, games and lots more at **www.capstonekids.com**

Author Bio

Children's author Jennifer Phillips dabbles in all things crafty. A southern Illinois native, Jennifer now calls Seattle home. She likes to write about artists and crafting when not working on her own projects. A member of the Society of Children's Book Writers and Illustrators, her children's work includes articles in *Highlights for Children*, *Learning through History*, and *Kiki* magazines and several books.

Snap Books are published by Capstone Press, 1710 Roe Crest Drive, North Mankato, Minnesota 56003. www.capstonepub.com

Library of Congress Cataloging-in-Publication Data
Phillips, Jennifer, 1962-
Adorable accessories: paper creations to wear / by Jennifer Phillips.
pages cm—(Snap books. Paper creations)
Includes bibliographical references and index.
Summary: "Step-by-step instructions teach readers how to make clothing and accessories with paper"—Provided by publisher.
ISBN 978-1-62065-043-1 (library binding)
ISBN 978-1-4765-1787-2 (eBook PDF)
1. Paper work—Juvenile literature. 2. Dress accessories—Juvenile literature. I. Title.
TT870.P493 2013
736'.98—dc23   2012020250

Editor: **Jennifer Besel**
Designer: **Tracy Davies McCabe**
Project and Photo Stylist: **Brent Bentrott**
Project Production: **Taylor Olson**
Prop Preparation: **Sarah Schuette**
Scheduler: **Marcy Morin**

Photo Credits:
All photos by Capstone Studio/Karon Dubke

Artistic Effects:
Shutterstock: fanny71, HAKKI ARSLAN, Itana, Labetskiy Alexandr Alexandrovich, Lichtmeister, mama-art, Marina Koven, Nils Z, Polina Katritch, vector-RGB

Printed in the United States of America in North Mankato, Minnesota.
092012   006933CGS13